KT-430-297

Airline Pilot

by Leonie Bennett

Editorial consultant: Mitch Cronick

ticktock

Copyright © **ticktock Entertainment Ltd 2006**
First published in Great Britain in 2006 by **ticktock Media Ltd.,**
Unit 2, Orchard Business Centre, North Farm Road, Tunbridge Wells, Kent TN2 3XF

We would like to thank: Shirley Bickler and Suzanne Baker

ISBN 1 86007 996 2 pbk
Printed in China

Picture credits
t=top, b=bottom, c=centre, l-left, r=right, OFC= outside front cover
AirTeamImages (Tomas Coelho): 15. BAA Aviation Photo Library: 11.
Cameron Bowerman: 20-21. Corbis: 4. The Flight Collection: 9, 10, 16, 17, 21t.
Brian Futterman: 19. Daniel Hamer: 12. John Kelly: 6–7.
Gary Lewis (ATCO Aviation photography): 13.

Every effort has been made to trace the copyright holders, and we apologise in advance for any
unintentional omissions. We would be pleased to insert the appropriate acknowledgements in any
subsequent edition of this publication.

CONTENTS

Words that look **bold like this** are in the glossary.

I'm an airline pilot

My name is Mike and I'm an airline pilot.

My job is exciting because I fly all over the world, but it is also hard work.

Today I am going to fly from London
to New York.

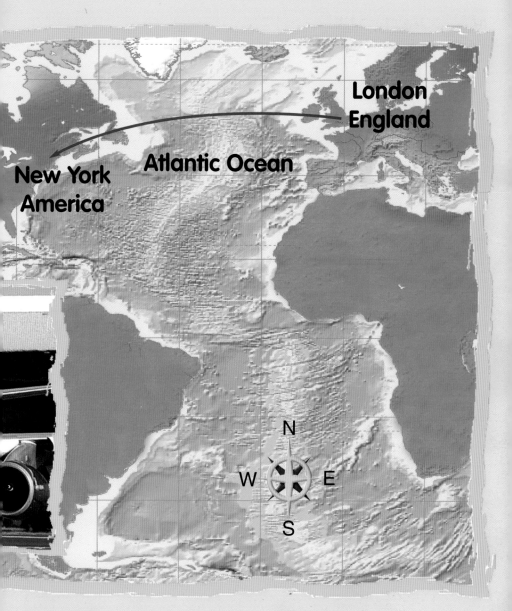

We will fly across the Atlantic Ocean.

The flight will take six hours.

Let's look at the plane

I fly a jumbo jet which is one of the biggest planes in the world.

Tail

Wing

Engine

Wheels

BRIT

It's got 188 windows and 18 wheels.

Its wings are so big you could park 45 cars on them!

Cockpit

Windows

Door

The pilot sits at the front, in the cockpit.

Checking the plane

I get to the airport early because there are lots of jobs to do.

First I must check the outside of the plane.

This is called the 'walk around'.

I check the wheels to make sure that the tyres are OK. Then I check the lights are working.

I look under the plane and in the engines. Sometimes dead birds get stuck there.

It is very important that everything is working properly.

Wheels

Preparing for take-off

A pilot never flies alone. There are always two pilots on every flight.

I am the captain on this flight and Don is the co-pilot. He will help me fly the plane.

Before taking off I check the **in-flight computer** and the **controls**.

Controls

I make sure everything is working.

Then I check the **weather forecast**.

Sunny

Rainy

Stormy

Snowy

Don checks the map to see the route we will take.

Map

Take-off

There are lots of planes waiting to take off.

Air traffic control will tell us when it is our turn.

When we have **permission** to take off we start going down the **runway.**

Runway

The plane speeds up. After 25 seconds it is going at 160 miles per hour.

Then it leaves the ground.

Wheels

When it is up in the air, the wheels go up into the plane.

Flight to America

We are on our way and the plane is flying at its **cruising speed** of 570 miles per hour.

We are flying above the clouds.

The passengers are watching films and listening to music.

Some of them are reading or sleeping.

The **flight attendants** give each passenger a meal.

The plane is full. There are 412 passengers on this plane.

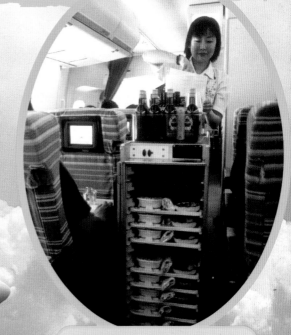

Flight attendant

Pilots at work

Don and I are working hard.

Don keeps talking to air traffic control. He checks the weather and the **fuel.**

I check what speed the plane is going and how high it is.

In-flight meal

The flight attendant brings us food and drinks in the cockpit.

We take it in turn to stop working and have something to eat.

Landing

We are getting near to New York so I ask air traffic control for permission to land.

Air traffic control

The weather is good but there are lots of other planes trying to land.

We fly around above the airport until it is our turn.

The wheels come down as we get ready to land.

Welcome to New York

When the plane touches down on the runway it is still going about 150 miles per hour.

The plane has strong brakes to slow it down.

Runway

At last the plane stops and the passengers get off. We have arrived in New York.

It was a good flight and everyone is happy. Tomorrow Don and I will fly back to London.

Passengers

Wheels down

Thinking and talking about pilots

What do the pilots do before take-off?

Why do the pilots need permission from air traffic control to take off and land?

Why do you think there are two pilots?

Would you like to be an airline pilot? Why or why not?

What do you think would be the best and worst things about being an airline pilot?

Glossary

air traffic control
People at the airport who tell the pilots when it is safe to taking off and land.

controls
These are used to fly the plane.

cruising speed
The steady speed that a plane flies at when it reaches its flying height.

flight attendants
People who look after the passengers on a plane.

fuel
Petrol or gas. Planes use a special kind of petrol.

in-flight computer
A computer that helps the pilots fly the plane.

permission
To be allowed to do something.

runway
A straight, wide road at an airport used by planes for taking off and landing.

weather forecast
A report that says what the weather will be like.